In Search of Cinderella

A Curriculum for the 21st Century
By Katharine Goodwin

Contents

In Search of Cinderella: A Curriculum for the 21st Century
Written by Katharine F. Goodwin
Cover Design by Andrea Miles
copyright ©2000 Shen's Books, Inc.
Shen's Books, Inc., 40951 Fremont Blvd., Fremont, CA 94538
800-456-6660 / www.shens.com
ISBN 1-885008-14-7 $15.95

ISBN 1-885008-14-7

51595

9 781885 008145

INTRODUCTION

The Cinderella story has been told for centuries in countries all over the world. Books have been written, classes have been held, seminars arranged, and arguments continued, discussing and analyzing the why and the how of this folklore happening. It is not really a surprising occurrence, because the story itself happens to be one that hits upon the twin factors of reality and magic in a way that touches the heart. And that truly is what the story is about. I have a friend who refuses to teach a unit on the Cinderella story (after years of doing so) after she began to reflect on the implications of teaching modern day young women about the possibility of being "rescued" or "saved" by a pie in the sky prince ... to say nothing of the fact that we try to teach all our children that beauty is not everything! I respect her ideas and recognize the validity of her connections but instead believe myself that we could do with a bit of magic and goodness winning out and use the stories to discuss the very points with which she takes issue. My sister is a Jungian analyst with a practice in South Africa and uses the Cinderella stories in her conferences about the collective unconscious and the importance of the hearth as symbol of home. I don't intend to pursue these lines of thought or argument or discussion, but instead will just list some of *my* reasons for using them in the classroom with young people:

- Everyone likes a good love story.

- There are many versions available and they are easy to locate.

- The stories can be used as a way to look at differences.

- The stories can be used as a way to look at similarities.

- These differences and similarities can be celebrated.

- Many versions follow the same simple plot that can be easily imitated.

- Social studies connections, creativity, and humor can be used as students write their own versions of the story.

- The tale can provide a way to use materials and methods that interest students as we teach them the skills needed to progress toward reading and writing proficiency and aim for meeting district, state, and national standards.

- The stories can provide an opportunity to discuss related topics:

    - gender issues (Do girls today ever sit around and wait for a prince of a fellow to appear?)
    - attitudes about beauty and appearance (Do we really get beyond these even today... why or why not?)
    - Cinderella versions that reveal young women who do take matters into their own hands (The movie *Ever After* is a video example of this ... just be aware that it is rated PG.)
    - values: honesty, trust, perseverance, duty, recognition of inner beauty, compassion, kindness, bravery
    - other curricular links: art, social studies, research, geography

USING & ADAPTING THESE LESSON PLANS

✻   Most of the plans are appropriate for the middle and upper grades, but could easily be adapted. Simply changing the format and giving more or less teacher guidance should make the lessons usable at a variety of grade levels. Feel free to adapt, enlarge, reduce, cut, paste, or use whiteout to make them your own.

✻   Just because these stories are illustrated, does not mean that they are necessarily for primary grades. Most fairy tales and folk stories that have been illustrated are told in language that most young children cannot read with real understanding. These sorts of stories are part of oral tradition and are meant to be read aloud. This includes the use by middle and upper grade students. The difference will be, that for older students, you may feel comfortable in using the books and the lesson plans in a small group format in which the *students* are doing the reading aloud within their group. A Degree of Reading Power (DRP) level is given for each of the Cinderella stories (see p.54) and this should give you an idea of the independent readability level of each of the stories.

✻   The **Booktalks** at the beginning of each section are meant for you as a teacher to use as a summary and quick review for yourself. But they may also be photo-copied and given to the students to use as they complete some of the lesson plans and projects after you have read the story aloud or after students have read the books aloud within groups. The first lesson plans for each story follow a similar format: a section on **Motifs and Ideas** for discussion; then a **Connection** to another aspect of the curriculum; and finally **Vocabulary Words** are listed (in alphabetical order to facilitate dictionary work) with either a cloze sentence or a matching section. The **Motifs and Ideas** section may include more hints, ideas, and events than some of you would like, but since each student will not have a copy of the book and all must listen to the story, I felt that more talking and predicting might help with comprehension. If you don't agree with this concept, simply fold back the top of the page before photocopying.

✻   The order in which you present the books is somewhat important, because the questions for some stories are based on other stories. For example, one of the lesson plans for *Cendrillon: The Caribbean Cinderella* presumes that students have read *The Persian Cinderella*. The **Answer Keys** at the end of the lesson plans also include tips on presenting the stories and on guiding students through some of the learning experiences. Within this **Introduction** section, there are lesson plans that can be used to introduce the project or serve as culminating activities. The **Self Evaluation** form may be used with any of the lesson plans that involve group work (the number of points can be changed with the use of whiteout!) as a means to assure accountability within the group.

LITERATURE TERMS & THE CINDERELLA STORIES

> Your teacher will assign one of the terms listed below for you to explain and teach to the class. Use the space below. Be prepared to present your work to the class or to a group. Suggestions: drawings, captions, charts, symbols, examples, poems, comic strip format ... anything that will help others understand better.

(part 1)

1. **character:** a person or animal who takes part in the action of a story

2. **character types**: recognizable, unchanging figures whom we meet over and over again in folk and fairy tales

3. **climax**: the turning point in a story; high point of interest or suspense

4. **conflict**: a struggle or clash (between characters or forces)

5. **fairy tale**: a tale which includes the use of magic

6. **folk tale**: a story passed on by word of mouth (oral tradition)

7. **foreshadowing**: hinting about something that will occur later in a story

8. **metamorphosis**: a marvelous change from one shape or form to another one

9. **motif**: a repeated element in storytelling

10. **oral tradition**: the passing of stories or poems by word of mouth from generation to generation

11. **plot**: sequence of events in a story

12. **point-of-view**: perspective from which a story is told

13. **resolution**: the point in a plot where the loose ends are tied up

14. **setting**: the time and place of a story

15. **suspense**: feeling of growing tension and excitement felt by a reader; anxiety about what will happen next in a story

16. **theme**: the idea about life revealed in a work of literature

Name _____ Class _____ Date _____

LITERATURE TERMS & THE CINDERELLA STORIES
(part 2)

> Take notes as your teacher and your class discuss the following literature terms. It will be helpful to write in an example for each.

1. character:

2. character types:

3. climax:

4. conflict:

5. fairy tale:

6. folk tale:

7. foreshadowing:

8. metamorphosis:

9. motif:

10. oral tradition:

11. plot:

12. point-of-view:

13. resolution:

14. setting:

15. suspense:

16. theme:

BINGO CARD

(part 1)

		FREE		

DIRECTIONS

1. Choose 24 answers. (The answers are the words printed in bold on BINGO: QUESTIONS/ANSWERS sheet.)

2. Write the answers to the 24 questions in the 24 squares above. Put them in any order you want. Do not leave any squares blank. Check off each answer as you put them on the Bingo Card so that you don't put the same answer in two squares.

3. Place a marker on any square containing an answer for a question that your teacher calls out. Call out "bingo" when a row is filled across, down, or diagonally.

Name _____ Class _____ Date _____

BINGO: QUESTIONS/ANSWERS

> Choose 24 answers and put them in the squares on your bingo card. The answers are the words written in bold.

(part 2)

1. Recognizable, unchanging figures in folk/fairy tales/**character types**
2. Hinting about something that may happen/**foreshadowing**
3. This Cinderella character dies and is brought back to life by the Spirit of Virtue/**Angkat**
4. She tells Cendrillon's story in the first person/**godmother**
5. The Cambodian Cinderella (Angkat) makes friends with a creature/**Little Fish**
6. A struggle or clash between opposing characters or forces/**conflict**
7. The perspective from which a story is told/**point of view**
8. A way of beginning to think about a story before reading/**predicting**
9. Retelling or simplifying a story in your own words/**summarizing**
10. This Cinderella story is one of the oldest known/**Yeh-Shen**
11. The idea about life revealed in a work of literature/**theme**
12. Yeh-Shen is a .... Cinderella story/**Chinese**
13. What is a thing an Algonquin girl sees and then marries/**The Invisible Being**
14. Domitila's wonderful .... first draws attention to herself/**cooking**
15. An Egyptian slave with "eyes as green as the Nile"/**Rhodopis**
16. The last part of the story where the problems are solved/**resolution**
17. Family members who mistreat a young girl is an example of this/**motif**
18. These are stories that are passed down by word of mouth/**folk tales**
19. Often the stepmother in Cinderella stories gives the girl many of these/**impossible tasks**
20. Settareh's name means .... in The Persian Cinderella/**star**
21. A fearsome woman in many of the Russian folk stories/**Baba Yaga**
22. Settareh loses an .... in the Cinderella tale from Persia/**anklet**
23. What is a symbol for the god Horus in The Egyptian Cinderella/**falcon**
24. Vasilisa, Cendrillon, and Jouanah are all helped by this/**mother's love**
25. The story Jouanah comes from the .... people of Southeast Asia/**Hmong**
26. A Zuni Cinderella story tells of a girl who was supposed to care for this/**turkeys**
27. Fairy tales usually include this/**magic**
28. Vasilisa's mother helps her by giving her a .... who is alive/**doll**
29. Domitila lives in an area of Mexico where there are many of these/**rancheros**
30. The series of events in a story/**plot**
31. Yeh-Shen, Jouanah, and Angkat are all helped by this magical creature/**fish**
32. This Cinderella tale has a sad ending/**The Turkey Girl**

Name _____ Class _____ Date _____

CREATING YOUR OWN CINDERELLA TALE
A Group Cinderella Book

DESCRIPTION

The simple plot and the use of motifs make this story one that is easy to imitate. There are hundreds of versions of the Cinderella tale that have been told and written over the years. The basic story is one that usually includes a young person whose mother dies leaving her in the care of a stepparent and stepsisters who are unkind and sometimes even jealous. There is often an event that the young person wants to attend, and then some help in making her look presentable. Often the help is magical. The central character is discovered (often by a prince or person of nobility,) and falls in love. Later there is a search for the owner of something (usually an article of clothing left behind,) and the young couple are reunited and married. Persons who are good and kind are rewarded and those who are not are punished, or at least do not get what they want.

Write and illustrate your own version of the Cinderella story. Think about setting, characters and events before you begin your first draft. Use the checklist below to make sure you have followed the writing process.

✍ have made a first draft

✍ first draft has been edited, revised, and checked for spelling, grammar, and punctuation

✍ included at least three Cinderella motifs

list them here:...

....

....

✍ there are illustrations with captions

✍ cover page includes a title and the names of students who worked on the project

✍ final writing is neat and has been reviewed by everyone in the group

Name _____ Class _____ Date _____

SELF EVALUATION
(Possible 40 points)

Evaluate yourself on the following points:

	Excellent	Satisfactory	Needs Improvement
Did I work well within the group?	☆	☆	☆
Did I put forth my best effort?	☆	☆	☆

List the specific parts that you worked on:

....

....

Circle the points you think you should earn:

    40 = excellent; I worked hard and did well

    30 = acceptable; I did my part

    20 = did not contribute as much as I should have

    10 = I did not help or contribute very much

Opinion of other group members:

    Name:..

      ☆   I agree with the above evaluation

      ☆   I disagree with the above evaluation

    Comments: ....

    Name:..

      ☆   I agree with the above evaluation

      ☆   I disagree with the above evaluation

    Comments: ....

    Name:..

      ☆   I agree with the above evaluation

      ☆   I disagree with the above evaluation

    Comments: ....

Abadeha
The Philippine Cinderella
Adapted by Myrna J. de la Paz/illustrated by Youshan Tang

Myrna J. de la Paz spent her childhood in the Philippines where she learned about traditional Filipino folklore. She retells this Cinderella tale in hopes that the rich indigenous pre-colonial lore of her people will not be lost after over 300 years of Spanish and American influence. Ms. De La Paz now makes her home in Los Angeles. Youshan Tang spent his childhood in China but now lives in San Francisco. A graduate of the Central Academy of fine Arts and Peking University with degrees in Chinese art and literature, Youshan recently illustrated another Cinderella tale for Shen's Books: *Anklet for a Princess: A Cinderella Story from India*.

As in most Cinderella tales, Abadeha is a young girl when her mother suddenly becomes ill and dies. Her fisherman father voyages to another island where he finds and marries a widow with two daughters. Abak brings the stepfamily home expecting that Abadeha will be cared for and cherished. Abadeha is mistreated and given the usual impossible tasks by a stepmother who threatens to whip her with the tail of a stingray. The sweet and hardworking girl is helped by the Spirit of the Forest who gives her a lovely sarimanok (a chicken with long flowing feathers). The cruel stepmother kills her pet and Abadeha is told to bury the bird's feet near her mother's grave. A magical tree grows from the spot and is covered with treasures. The son of the island chieftain comes upon the tree and tries on a ring which causes his finger to swell so that it cannot be removed. The prince dreams that a young girl who springs from an orchid removes the ring. When he awakens, the search for the lovely and kind girl begins and eventually, with the help of the Spirit of the Forest, Abadeha is able to meet the prince and remove the ring.

Abadeha wears a golden gown and jewelry from the enchanted tree and her father arrives home from his fishing trip in time for the wedding. Stepmother and her daughters are banished to the chicken yard. The tale ends with marriage and the message that the prince and his bride share their wealth and happiness with their people.

Name _____ Class _____ Date _____

Abadeha
The Philippine Cinderella
Adapted by Myrna J. de la Paz/illustrated by Youshan Tang

MOTIFS AND IDEAS

📖 Abadeha's father is a fisherman; story contains many island images

📖 mother dies; father remarries a widow with two daughters

📖 when daughter is mistreated, she is helped by the Spirit of the Forest

📖 as in some Asian Cinderella stories, a beloved pet (this time a sarimanok) is killed by the stepmother

📖 an enchanted tree grows from the bird's feet which Abadeha has buried near her mother's grave

📖 the prince is the son of the island chieftain

📖 a dream leads the prince to his future wife who removes a ring from his finger

CONNECTIONS

The title page of *Abadeha* is done in an ancient and almost forgotten type of writing called Alebata. Using the Internet, key in *Alebata* to learn more about this language. Use the space below to write about what you find.

VOCABULARY WORDS

pleaded	betel	ancestors	laden
sarimanok	radiant	hammock	commotion
carefree	mock	ritual	solace

Choose the word that matches the meaning:

1. ...... a hanging bed made of ropes or canvas   a. solace

2. ...... orange-colored nuts from an Asian tree   b. mock

3. ...... consolation or comfort   c. betel

4. ...... persons from whom one is descended   d. hammock

5. ...... bright or shining   e. ancestors

6. ...... to ridicule or make fun of   f. radiant

Name _____ Class _____ Date _____

Abadeha
The Philippine Cinderella
Adapted by Myrna J. de la Paz/illustrated by Youshan Tang

QUICKWRITE
In *Abadeha* there is an enchanted tree and on the tree are rings, bracelets, necklaces, earrings, jewels, and gowns. Write about what would hang on your enchanted tree (if you had one!):

....

....

....

....

VISUALIZE IT
Draw your enchanted tree. Underneath your drawing write a caption that summarizes the illustration.

Abadeha
The Philippine Cinderella
Adapted by Myrna J. de la Paz/illustrated by Youshan Tang

A **CHARACTER** is a person or animal who takes part in the action of a story.

Example: the wolf in "The Three Little Pigs."

CHARACTER TYPES are recognizable, unchanging figures who we meet over and over again in folk and fairy tales.

Example: the "antagonist" or the "evil one" ... the one the hero or heroine must overcome to fulfill a mission or a task.

Directions: Sort the following characters from some of the Cinderella stories you are familiar with into the proper **character types.**

Angkat in *Angkat*

the **falcon** in *The Egyptian Cinderella*

Spirit of the Forest in *Abadeha*

Domitila in *Domitila*

the **godmother** (Nannin') in *Cendrillon*

The Old One in *The Turkey Girl*

the **invisible warrior** in *Sootface*

Baba Yaga in *Vasilissa the Beautiful*

The son of the island chieftain in *Abadeha*

the **pari** in *The Persian Cinderella*

Shee-Nang in *Jouanah*

Settareh in *The Persian Cinderella*

Abadeha in *Abadeha*

the **magistrate** in *The Korean Cinderella*

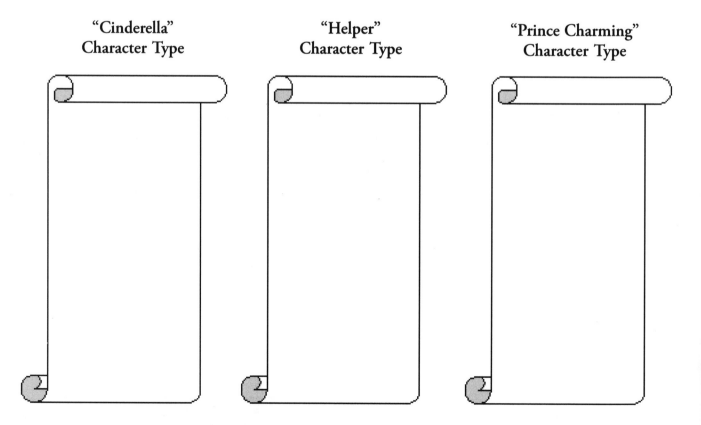

"Cinderella" Character Type   "Helper" Character Type   "Prince Charming" Character Type

Angkat
A Cambodian Cinderella
by Jewell Reinhart Coburn / illustrated by Eddie Flotte

Dr. Jewell Reinhart Coburn is the highly respected author of books on storytelling and folklore, as well as several children's books, including *Jouanah: A Hmong Cinderella*. She found an 18th century version of Angkat while researching Khmer culture and history and this provided the basis for The Cambodian Cinderella. The Khmer culture has had a strong influence on Cambodia where it has existed for almost 6000 years. Eddie Flotte's watercolor illustrations not only support and enhance the storyteller's vision, but also provide authentic representations of ancient Cambodian architecture, clothing, and symbolically, of these peoples' belief in the spirit world.

A lonely, widowed fisherman lives in Cambodia with his dutiful daughter Angkat. He meets and marries a widow who has a daughter who is beautiful on the outside but soon causes problems within the family by insisting that she should have the honor of being Number One child rather than Angkat. A fishing contest is arranged between the two girls and Kantok steals three of her stepsister's fish, thereby leaving Angkat to become the Number Two daughter destined to always be the family servant. Angkat frees her remaining fish but later befriends Little Fish when she discovers that it is magical. Kantok discovers the friendship and kills Little Fish but the Spirit of Virtue tells Angkat to leave the Little Fish's bones under her mat where they turn into golden slippers. When a huge black bird brings one of the slippers to the Prince, this provides an opportunity for the couple to eventually meet after the traditional search for the owner of the slipper.

In this story, the tale doesn't end with the marriage ceremony as Angkat's jealous family (including her father!) conspire to kill her and allow Kantok to take her place in the palace. After Angkat's death, the Spirit of Virtue reunites the couple in the sweet breezes of a bamboo grove and brings Angkat back to life. The scheming family is banished forever from Cambodia and the royal couple reign joyfully over a peaceful kingdom for many years.

Angkat
The Cambodian Cinderella
by Jewell Reinhart Coburn / illustrated by Eddie Flotte

MOTIFS AND IDEAS

📖 Angkat's father marries a cruel woman with a beautiful but cruel daughter

📖 like Yeh-Shen, Angkat is befriended by a fish who is killed; the Spirit of Virtue helps Angkat and turns bones into slippers

📖 bird takes slipper to the Prince and the search is on

📖 Angkat and the Prince marry but she is killed

📖 Angkat returns to life

CONNECTIONS
Using atlases, encyclopedias, and/or Internet websites, research the following:

★ find Cambodia on a map ★ list countries surrounding Cambodia

★ Temple ruins of Angkor ★ traditional clothing of Cambodia

★ Khmer architecture ★ fish and animals of Cambodia

VOCABULARY WORDS

bamboo	dawdle(d)	iridescent	sampot
banished	destiny	multitude	sarong
concoct(ed)	hoist(ed)	mystical	summon(ed)
dallied	inlet	prosperity	trekked

Choose the word that matches its meaning:

1. .... long wrapped article of clothing   a. sampot

2. .... to raise or lift   b. dawdle(d)

3. .... fate; predetermined course of events   c. iridescent

4. .... a way into the sea or ocean or lake   d. hoist(ed)

5. .... to devise or plan; to cook up   e. banish(ed)

6. .... Cambodian jacket-like clothing   f. destiny

7. .... a great number   g. mystical

8. .... spiritual meaning or reality   h. inlet

9. .... to spend time idly; waste time   i. multitude

10. .... to drive away from home or a country   j. sarong

11. .... a rainbow like array of colors   k concoct(ed)

Name _____ Class _____ Date_____

Angkat
The Cambodian Cinderella
by Jewell Reinhart Coburn / illustrated by Eddie Flotte

ADVERB: a word used to modify a verb, an adjective, or another adverb; adverbs often end in ly (for example, kindly)

PREPOSITION: a word used to show the relationship of a noun or pronoun to another word in the sentence (for example, with)

PRONOUN: a word used in place of a noun or more than one noun (for example, she)

Sort each italicized word from Angkat into the correct column according to how it is used in the phrase.

I am entitled	slipped *gracefully*	*his* daughter	*in* the family
She picked	*to* herself	skipped *lightly*	*to* the pond
will await *you*	*carefully* followed	*he* had said	*her* feathered friends
under her mat	Come here *quickly*	*My* search	died *instantly*
They put on	*without* a wife	rid of *it*	blessed them *abundantly*
banished *forever*	*by* the Spirit	*with* the biggest fish	

ADVERB   **PREPOSITION**   **PRONOUN**

Angkat
The Cambodian Cinderella
by Jewell Reinhart Coburn / illustrated by Eddie Flotte

PREPOSITIONAL POEM — a poem written in a format in which every line (or almost every line) begins with a preposition.

1. Write a prepositional poem about Angkat after thinking about the important characters and events.

2. The poem below is an example of a prepositional poem and is about the main character in *The Persian Cinderella*.

> *Settareh*
> *Under the stars*
> *Outside the palace*
> *After help from her pari*
> *With hungry heart,*
> *And flowing scarf*
> *Over her face,*
> *And jewels*
> *Round her ankles ...*
> *She met her Prince*
> *Mehrdad.*

3. Some prepositions to help you start:

at, above, across, against, around, before, behind, below, beneath, from, in, inside, into, near, on, out, of, over, past, since, through, to, toward, under, without

Anklet For a Princess
A Cinderella Story from India
Story by Lila Mehta/Adapted by Meredith Brucker/illustrated by Youshan Tang

Lila Mehta was born in India and educated in England and now teaches in Canada. Her story is based on oral tradition and includes centuries-old beliefs that snakes were powerful underwater creatures that could reward or punish. Meridith Babeaux Brucker is an editor and writer who graduated from Stanford University and now lives in Southern California. Artist Youshan Tang was educated in China and now makes his home in San Francisco. He also illustrated *Abadeha: The Philippine Cinderella* for Shen's books. In *Anklet for a Princess*, Tang's watercolor illustrations are full of the vivid colors and musical movements of ancient India.

As usual in these Cinderella tales, there is a young girl who has lost her mother and who is mistreated by a stepmother. Cinduri has lost not only her mother, but also her father, and has been left with her father's second wife and stepsister Lata. One day when Cinduri is making one of her daily trips to the lake for water, she is visited by a great white snake who questions why she is dressed in rags and looking so hungry. The white snake adopts her, teaches her a magic song, and eventually gives her a brilliant red jewel so that she can dress herself beautifully enough to attend the Navarati Festival. When Cinduri arrives at the festival, she attracts the attention of the Prince of Suryanagar when she dances imitating the movements of her Godfather Snake. She must leave by midnight and when she departs suddenly, she loses one of her anklets made with bells and diamonds.

The prince travels about searching for the owner of the tiny anklet and eventually finds his true love. There is a wedding celebration with garlands of white jasmine flowers and Cinduri and the Prince move to a palace built by his father. A pond is built so that Godfather Snake can come to live nearby but Cinduri's stepmother and stepsister are banished to wander as beggars when they are not willing to work hard enough to keep their home in the village. The tale ends with a promise of happy days and a thank you from Cinduri to her Godfather Snake.

Name _____ Class _____ Date _____

Anklet for a Princess
A Cinderella Story from India
Story by Lila Mehta /Adapted by Meredith Brucker/illustrated by Youshan Tang

MOTIFS AND IDEAS

- in this story both parents have died
- Cinduri is mistreated by her father's second wife who has become her stepmother
- the young girl's beauty, hard work, and politeness impress a powerful snake
- Godfather Snake becomes Cinduri's helper
- Magical elements include a song and a jewel
- Cinduri wears and loses an anklet instead of a shoe or slipper
- Godfather Snake comes to live with the happy couple in a pond near their palace

CONNECTIONS

Cinduri meets her prince on the ninth day of a harvest celebration called the Navaratri Festival. Research what peoples or countries celebrate the following harvest festivals:

Yam Festival................ Succoth................. Pongal.................

Thanksgiving................. Harvest Home................. Hounen Odori.................

Crop Over (Sugar Cane)................. Birthday of the Moon.................

Answers include: India; United States of America & Canada; British Isles; Ghana & Nigeria; Japan; Israel; Barbados; China

VOCABULARY WORDS

tantalizing	sputter	stammered	marquee
aromas	pavilion	miraculous	conch
cholera	pomegranate	sari	fetch

Choose the word that matches the meaning:

1. ...... a reddish fruit with many seeds and a sour taste   a. sputter
2. ...... a rooflike shelter over an entrance   b. sari
3. ...... to talk excitedly and with confusion   c. pomegranate
4. ...... pleasantly spicy odors or smells   d. fetch
5. ...... the outer garment or dress of Hindu women   e. conch
6. ...... a large spiral shell   f. aromas
7. ...... to go and get; bring   g. marquee

Name _____ Class _____ Date_____

Anklet for a Princess
A Cinderella Story from India
Story by Lila Mehta /Adapted by Meredith Brucker/illustrated by Youshan Tang

QUICKWRITE

Before you read or listen to the book, look at the illustration on the cover and list three things you notice about it:

1. ....

2. ....

3. ....

After reading (or listening to) the story:

CLARIFY

Write words or ideas from this book that you need to discuss with your teacher and classmates:

....

....

....

QUESTION

Write one question about this book. Start your question with one of these words: Why, Who, When, What, or Where. ....

....

PREDICT

Predict (guess) what will happen next: ....

....

SUMMARIZE

Briefly tell what happened in this story: ....

....

....

....

....

....

....

Name _____   Class _____   Date _____

Anklet for a Princess
A Cinderella Story from India
Story by Lila Mehta /Adapted by Meredith Brucker/illustrated by Youshan Tang

LEARNING TO RESEARCH

The author of *Anklet for a Princess* does not describe Godfather Snake in detail. However she does give hints that the snake who helps Cinduri is a cobra and the illustrator pictures Godfather Snake as a large king cobra. Find three facts about king cobras and list them below. Then write where you found those facts. Good research involves using <u>more than one source</u> and <u>a variety of formats</u>. Check out the following for some examples of how to cite sources: <http://www.monroe.lib.in.us/childrens/cite.html> or <kidsconnect.org>

<u>Source</u>:   anyplace you find information

<u>Format</u>;   print (such as an encyclopedia, magazine, newspaper, or book)

               interview (with an expert in the field)

               electronic (a CD-ROM, an online database, or the Internet)

THREE FACTS ABOUT KING COBRA

```
┌─────────────────────────────────────┐
│                                      │
│                                      │
│                                      │
└─────────────────────────────────────┘
```

```
┌─────────────────────────────────────┐
│                                      │
│                                      │
│                                      │
└─────────────────────────────────────┘
```

```
┌─────────────────────────────────────┐
│                                      │
│                                      │
│                                      │
└─────────────────────────────────────┘
```

WHERE I FOUND THESE FACTS

```
┌─────────────────────────────────────┐
│                                      │
│                                      │
│                                      │
│                                      │
└─────────────────────────────────────┘
```

Baba Yaga and Vasilisa the Brave
as told by Marianna Mayer / illustrated by K.Y.Craft

Marianna Mayer and Kinuko Y. Craft also wrote and illustrated the highly praised book *The Twelve Dancing Princesses*. Both books are rich in their illustrations and faithful to the traditions that the stories reveal. Students will appreciate the intricate borders around the watercolor, gouache, and oil paintings that illuminate each page.

Baba Yaga is introduced as a terrible character from Russian folktales who lives alone in the forest and likes to eat humans. Vasilisa is kind and beautiful and lives with her stepmother and stepsister after the death of her father. An unusual aspect of this tale is that her mother has left Vasilisa a concrete symbol of her love in the form of a doll who is actually alive. The stepmother devises a sinister plot to rid her homely and dull-witted daughters of their kind stepsister by sending Vasilisa on an errand to ask for a light from Baba Yaga. On the way to the fearsome old lady's house made of bones, Vasilisa meets three horsemen who represent daybreak, sun, and night. Baba Yaga promises Vasilisa a light but requires her to perform tasks to prove her worth. The tasks are impossible ones but Vasilisa's tiny doll helps her to complete them. When Vasilisa answers Baba Yaga's question as to how she managed to complete the tasks and says, "By my mother's love," the wicked old woman has had enough of her, and sends her on her way with a light inside a skull. When Vasilisa arrives home, the magical skull destroys the stepmother and two stepsisters.

Vasilisa is on her own now, but is soon taken in by a kind elderly woman who teaches her how to spin and weave. The beautiful fabric that she creates is eventually shown to the tzar who wishes to see the person who wove it. Of course once he has set eyes on Vasilisa, he asks her to marry him. The story ends with a magnificent wedding, a feast, and a reflection on how Vasilisa keeps the little doll and her memories of Baba Yaga for the rest of her life.

Name _____ Class _____ Date _____

Baba Yaga and Vasilisa the Brave
as told by Marianna Mayer / illustrated by K.Y.Craft

MOTIFS AND IDEAS

📖 mother dies but leaves Vasilisa a gift of love—a doll she has made for her

📖 father remarries and Vasilisa has a stepmother and two stepsisters

📖 father dies and mistreatment gets worse

📖 two older persons (one of the older women, Baba Yaga, is scary) and a magic doll help Vasilisa; three horsemen representing daybreak, sun, and night

📖 a test of worthiness but no ball or festival

📖 a wedding to the tsar at the end

CONNECTIONS

Baba Yaga is a character found in many Russian folk stories. She is an old woman who has a frightening appearance and who is obviously cruel, but sometimes is willing to give help. Baba Yaga has an enormous appetite and in this story Vasilisa prepares two delicious meals for Baba Yaga as part of her test of worthiness. As your teacher reads the story aloud to you, listen for context clues and write down what each Russian food word means:

blinis ....

borscht ....

piroshki ....

shchi ....

coulibiac ....

VOCABULARY WORDS

chaff	gruesome	menial	sinister
compassionate	idle	mortar & pestle	tzar
embers	incessant	ravenous	whim

Choose the word that matches its meaning:

1. .... showing compassion or sympathy   a. mortar & pestle

2. .... horrible; inspiring horror   b. idle

3. .... evil; from Latin meaning left-sided   c. compassionate

4. .... inactive, not busy   d. whim

5. .... seed coverings; worthless   e. tzar

6. .... very hungry; eager for food   f. gruesome

7. .... a sudden idea or fancy   g. menial

8. .... relating to a servant; humble   h. sinister

9. .... emperor; ruler of Russia   i. chaff

10. .... container & something to pound with   j. ravenous

Name _____   Class _____   Date _____

Baba Yaga and Vasilisa the Brave
as told by Marianna Mayer / illustrated by K.Y.Craft

1. After reading or listening to *Baba Yaga & Vasilisa the Brave*, complete the information below.

2. The "I thought ..." section should be written in complete sentences and you should use every line.

3. In the area at the bottom of the page, draw an illustration with a caption (words explaining the picture) of something that interested you from the story.

Country or Ethnic Group: ....

Hero or Heroine: ....

Description of family: ....

A conflict or hardship: ....

Event helper: ....

Test of worthiness: ....

Use of magic: ....

Resolution: ....

I thought this story: ....

....

....

....

....

Baba Yaga and Vasilisa the Brave
as told by Marianna Mayer / illustrated by K.Y.Craft

PLOT — the sequence of events in a story; it can include:

1. introduction or exposition: tells the setting of the story, who the major characters are, and what their conflict is
2. rising action or complications: actions taken to solve the problem or conflict
3. climax: the high point of the story; most suspenseful or emotional point in the plot when the outcome is decided
4. falling action: the part of the plot when the story begins to draw to a close
5. resolution: the character's problems are solved and the story ends

---

After listening to *Baba Yaga and Vasilisa the Brave* list the following events in the plot under the correct heading.

- ☆ an elderly woman takes Vasilisa into her home
- ☆ Baba Yaga is introduced on the 1st page
- ☆ Vasilisa sees the three horsemen
- ☆ Vasilisa completes all the tasks given her
- ☆ the main character's family are described
- ☆ the tzar sends for the person who made the cloth
- ☆ the stepmother and stepsisters are destroyed
- ☆ Vasilisa learns to spin and weave
- ☆ we learn about the doll
- ☆ Vasilisa marries the tzar
- ☆ Baba Yaga gives the skull to Vasilisa
- ☆ the stepmother sends Vasilisa for light
- ☆ the doll helps Vasilisa with her tasks
- ☆ Vasilisa finds Baba Yaga's house

Introduction..

....

....

Rising Action ....

....

Climax ....

Falling Action..

....

....

Resolution...

Cendrillon
A Caribbean Cinderella
by Robert San Souci / illustrated by Brian Pinkney

Robert D. San Souci is the award-winning author of well-known tales such as *The Talking Eggs*, *The Faithful Friend*, and *Sukey and the Mermaid*. One of his most recent books is a retelling of the Tarzan story that is much closer to the Edgar Rice Burroughs original than other modern retellings. His attention to researched details and his ability to capture and reproduce the mood of the oral storyteller make his folktales faithful to the genre. Caldecott Award winner Brian Pinkney illustrates Cendrillon using his trademark scratchboard, luma dyes, gouache, and oil paints, creating a visual feast of bright Caribbean colors that bring the story to life.

Cendrillon is different from most other Cinderella motif folktales in that it is told in the first person. The teller of this Creole story set on the Caribbean island of Martinique is a poor and loving godmother whose only magical tool is a mahogany wand left by her mother before she died. The storyteller works for a kind but sickly woman who appreciates her hardworking servant and makes her godmother (nannin') of her baby girl, Cendrillon, before she dies. The story reveals that on this Caribbean island there is a social class system whereby anyone French is held in high esteem. Robert San Souci uses many French Creole words and phrases but they are woven into the tale with use of context clues and therefore add flavor rather than distraction. After the death of Cendrillon's mother, her father remarries and there is the usual story of a woman who mistreats her stepdaughter and spoils Vitaline, her own daughter. With the help of her magical wand, Nannin' makes it possible for Cendrillon to attend a birthday fet' for a handsome, well spoken and kind young man called Paul.

There is a missed deadline and the loss of a slipper, but in the end, Cendrillon is recognized by her true-love despite her refusal of any more magical help from her godmother. Nannin' celebrates the wedding with dancing and nine helpings of chocolate sherbet!

Cendrillon
A Caribbean Cinderella
by Robert San Souci / illustrated by Brian Pinkney

MOTIFS AND IDEAS

- 📖 kind mother dies after making her washerwoman the baby's godmother
- 📖 narrated in the first person by Cendrillon's godmother, who uses a magic wand to help her
- 📖 father remarries; half-sister is born; Cendrillon is mistreated
- 📖 many French Creole words are used and explained
- 📖 lovely clothing, and a slipper
- 📖 ends with wedding and "true-love"

CONNECTIONS

In the beginning of the story, the narrator tells of her wand of mahogany and how it can work its magic only for a short time and only to help someone she loves. Love is sometimes described as magical. Think and write about how the ideas love and magic could be connected:

....

....

....

....

....

VOCABULARY WORDS

astonishing	chaperone	mahogany	peasant
breadfruit	chimes	manioc	sherbert
calico	christening	Martinique	shoulder-scarf
Caribbean Sea	commotion	pallet	washerwoman

Choose the word that matches its meaning:

1. .... an edible plant   a. Martinique
2. .... an inexpensive cotton fabric   b. mahogany
3. .... a water area east of Central America   c. christening
4. .... person who accompanies a young girl   d. Caribbean Sea
5. .... ceremony for baptizing & naming a child   e. manioc
6. .... a French West Indies island   f. calico
7. .... wood from a hard durable West Indian tree   g. peasant
8. .... a person of a low social class; a laborer   h. chaperone

Name _____   Class _____   Date _____

Cendrillon
A Caribbean Cinderella
by Robert San Souci / illustrated by Brian Pinkney

QUICKWRITE

In this Cinderella story, there are many French Creole words and phrases that are explained through context clues. Give an example of a context clue:

....

....

CLARIFY

When your teacher stops reading, write one word or an idea that you need explained:

....

....

QUESTION

Write one question about the story: (Begin with one of these words: Why, Who, When, What, Where)

....

....

....

PREDICT

After your teacher reads the part where Cendrillon's godmother meets her at the river and asks, "What troubles you so, my child?" Predict what will happen next:

....

....

SUMMARIZE

When you have finished listening to (or reading) the story, write a one-paragraph summary of the story. Include the setting, main characters, what happened (the plot), and the ending or resolution of the story. Use complete sentences:

....

....

....

....

EVALUATE

What did you like best about this Cinderella story?

....

....

....

Name _____ Class _____ Date _____

Cendrillon
A Caribbean Cinderella
by Robert San Souci / illustrated by Brian Pinkney

> Use the Venn diagram below to compare and contrast *Cendrillon* with *The Persian Cinderella*. In each of the two labeled circles, list items, events, characters, and locations that apply to that tale. In the intersecting sections, list things that apply to both stories. When you are finished, make a border around each circle that includes symbols or items from that story. (Examples: *The Persian Cinderella* — repetitive Persian designs; turtledoves; shapes of buildings. *Cendrillon* — Caribbean plants and flowers; jewelry; ocean and sky symbols.)

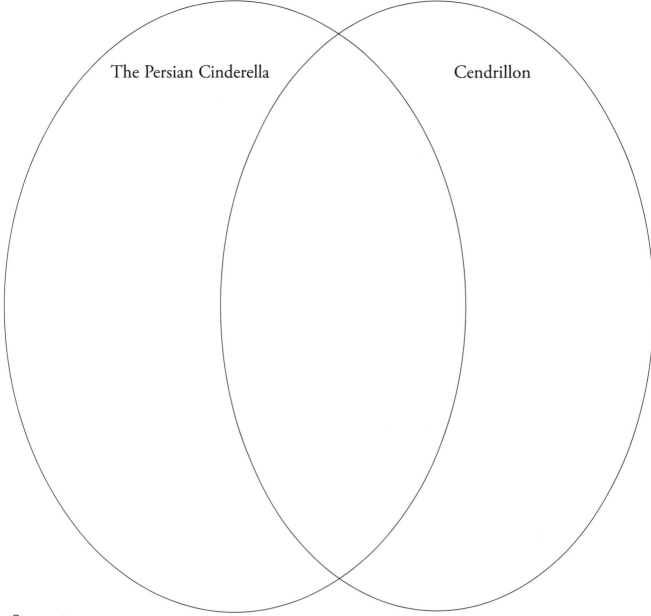

The Persian Cinderella

Cendrillon

Suggestions:

✯ artwork ✯ heroine ✯ death ✯ location ✯ clothes ✯ lost article of clothing ✯ who helps the heroine ✯ headwear ✯ half or stepsister(s) ✯ other family members ✯ magical objects ✯ ending ✯ character traits ✯ language ✯ use of spells ✯ food ✯ description of father

Domitila
A Cinderella Tale from the Mexican Tradition
adapted by Jewell Reinhart Coburn / illustrated by Connie McLennan

The author of Domitila knows well the many versions of the Cinderella tale that are told in lands around the world. Dr. Coburn has retold two of these stories (*Jouanah: A Hmong Cinderella*, and *Angkat: The Cambodian Cinderella*.) In *Domitila* she sets her story far away in time and place from those tales of southwest Asia. She writes of a young girl living on a rancho in a sun-scorched area of Mexico softened by the beauty of the desert and shadowed by the majestic Sierra Madre mountains. Connie McLennan captures the loveliness of the area and the warmth of the people in the vibrant colors of her oil paintings. Details of life on the rancho, from the way the adobe homes are built to the fiestas that center on mouth-watering and aromatic foods, are captured in the words and the illustrations of the author and illustrator. Spanish and Mexican proverbs (written both in Spanish and English) along with patterns, symbols, and artifacts that represent the culture frame the story page by page.

Domitila is a loving and beloved daughter who learns from and helps her parents in many ways. She has learned to cook delicious dishes, has assisted in the making of bricks and the building of their adobe casa, and creates intricate designs on the leather-goods produced by the family. When the family home and garden are destroyed by a violent rainstorm, Domitila willingly goes off to earn money by working in the kitchen of the Governor of Hidalgo. The handsome but egotistical eldest son falls in love with Domitila, but for her cooking and leather-making skills rather than her beauty. When Domitila leaves the mansion to return home to her sick mother, Timoteo follows her with only a scrap of finely carved leather from Domitila's sandal and the knowledge of her fine cooking to help him as he searches the rancho country.

In the meantime, Domitila must face life without her loving mother who dies before she reaches home, but whose spirit appears to her and gives her words of support. The father remarries and there is the usual mistreatment by a scheming stepmother and cruel stepsister but eventually Timoteo finds Domitila and is transformed not only by her cooking and talents but by her inner goodness. After placing his abuela's lovely shawl around her shoulders, they set off for the capital of Hidalgo where Domitila becomes the bride of the future Governor. The wicked stepmother and sister flee, but Domitila's father joins her in her new life with a husband who has learned kindness from his wife.

Domitila
A Cinderella Tale from the Mexican Tradition
adapted by Jewell Reinhart Coburn / illustrated by Connie McLennan

MOTIFS AND IDEAS
- Hildalgo, a desert ranching area of Mexico
- Domitila, a very capable young woman who does not need magic
- the "prince", the son of the Governor who is selfish and rude
- a sandal strap and a shawl
- the spirit of Domitila's mother
- at the "Fiesta" Timoteo learns more of Domitila
- stepmother and stepsister trick Timoteo
- love transforms Timoteo

CONNECTIONS
In many tales, food is an important part of the story. People everywhere place importance on eating and on delicious food and often the message of the story is connected to food or to a meal. For example, in the Goldilocks story the eating of the porridge is a major part of the plot. List and explain some other stories in which food is important:

....

....

....

VOCABULARY WORDS

abuela	contrite	fragrance	plight
arrogant	cunning	mansion	pondered
buenos dias	deeds	nopales	serape
casa	exquisitely	passed away	smirk

Choose the word that matches the meaning:

1. .... a way of saying that someone died   a. deeds

2. .... Spanish for "good day"   b. serape

3. .... Spanish for "house"   c. passed away

4. .... actions; something a person does   d. abuela

5. .... a shawl worn as an outer garment   e. cunning

6. .... using slyness or trickery   f. smirk

7. .... Spanish for grandmother   g. casa

8. .... to smile in a smug or affected way   h. buenos dias

Name_____ Class_____ Date_____

Domitila
A Cinderella Tale from the Mexican Tradition
adapted by Jewell Reinhart Coburn / illustrated by Connie McLennan

PROVERB — a short saying that expresses a thought or a moral about what many people believe to be true. In this story from the Mexican tradition, there is a proverb written in the border of each page of the book. These popular sayings express beliefs held by the narrator and the characters in the tale. Many of these proverbs are universal — they are beliefs held by many peoples in different cultures around the world.

1. Choose one of the proverbs listed below from Domitila.

2. Circle it, and draw a picture that illustrates or shows the meaning of the words.

3. Write the proverb that you have chosen at the bottom of your illustration to complete the assignment.

Love is the very best food for the soul. *(El amor es el mejor alimento para el alma.)*

Selfishness often injures the person who displays it. *(El egoismo a menudo hiere a la persona que lo demuestra.)*

Love is not easily discouraged. *(Al amor no se le desalienta facilmente.)*

Deeds, more than words, are proof of love. *(Obras son amores y no buenas razones.)*

Domitila
A Cinderella Tale from the Mexican Tradition
adapted by Jewell Reinhart Coburn / illustrated by Connie McLennan

ANALOGY — an analogy begins with two words or items that are related to each other. You must figure out what that relationship is and then complete another pair that has the same relationship.

Example: *Hot* is to *cold* as *warm* is to ....

Your Answer: **cool**

Choose a word from the list below that best completes each analogy.

shawl	contrite	arrogant	fiesta	mansion	good day
Timoteo	mountains	kind	tortillas	Mexico	fragrance

1. *Cinderella* is to *Domitila* as *Prince* is to ....

2. *Buenos noches* is to *good night* as *buenos dias* is to ....

3. *Church* is to *cathedral* as *house* is to ....

4. *Mississippi* is to river as *Sierra Madre* is to ....

5. *Cactus* is to *nopales* as *party* is to ....

6. *Humble* is to *meek* as *proud* is to ....

7. *Shoes* are to *sandals* as *bread* is to ....

8. *Malvina* is to *cunning* as *Domitila* is to ....

9. *California* is to *United States* as *Hildalgo* is to ....

10. *Leather* is to Domitila's *sandals* as *silk* is to Abuela's..

The Egyptian Cinderella
by Shirley Climo / illustrated by Ruth Heller

The author has retold three other Cinderella stories: *The Irish Cinderlad*, *The Korean Cinderella*, and *The Persian Cinderella*. She carefully chooses just the right verb, noun, or adjective to make the reader truly visualize the characters and happenings of the stories. Ruth Heller's bright illustrations provide a feast of colors and carefully researched images. The Author's Note tells us that this Cinderella tale is one of the oldest recorded. It was written down by a Roman historian in the first century B.C. History tells us that the tale is based on some true events as the Pharaoh Amasis did marry a Greek slave girl named Rhodopis in the fifth century B.C.

A young girl named Rhodopis is kidnapped and taken away from her home in Greece. She is sold as a slave to a kind but elderly Egyptian man who never seems to notice her mistreatment by the household servants. Her name means "rosy-cheeked" because her skin is burned red from the hot Egyptian sun while the other girls have dark and coppery skin. Rhodopis befriends the animals and, despite her hard life, finds joy in singing and dancing. One day when her master sees her dancing joyfully, he rewards her with a pair of lovely rose-red slippers gilded with gold. Although Rhodopis is not taken along to see the Pharaoh when he holds court for all his subjects, she gains the Pharaoh's attention when one of her tiny slippers is stolen by a great falcon, symbol of the god Horus. The bird drops the tiny slipper onto the lap of a bored and yawning Pharaoh who is holding court. Amasis is determined to find the owner of the slipper and, of course, the search eventually leads him to Rhodopis who is able to show him the shoe's mate.

The tale ends with a comment by the Pharaoh that shows that even in ancient times, when slavery was common, and there was little acceptance of class differences, the beginnings of tolerance were present when a pharaoh dared to marry a slave. Amasis describes Rhodopis as "the most Egyptian of all ... for her eyes are as green as the Nile, her hair as feathery as papyrus, and her skin the pink of a lotus flower."

Name _____ Class _____ Date _____

The Egyptian Cinderella
by Shirley Climo / illustrated by Ruth Heller

MOTIFS AND IDEAS

📖 Rhodopis, "rosy cheeked," is a slave girl with no family or friends

📖 she is mistreated by the servant girls who make fun of her

📖 friends with animals like the ones found in *Yeh-Shen, Turkey Girl*, and *Angkat*

📖 her master admires her tiny feet and gives her slippers

📖 falcon steals one slipper and gives it to the Pharaoh

📖 Pharaoh searches for owner of slipper

📖 Rhodopis becomes Pharaoh's queen

CONNECTIONS

Using atlases, encyclopedias, and/or Internet websites, research the following:

☆ why all the faces in the story are in profile   ☆ clothing of the Egyptians

☆ Horus, Egyptian sky god   ☆ Nile River Valley

☆ papyrus   ☆ Egyptian jewelry

VOCABULARY WORDS

barge	gilded	Memphis	soar
coaxed	heed	nimble	summoned
din	linen	papyrus	talons
gawked	maiden	scoffed	tunic

Choose the word that matches its meaning:

1. .... flat-bottomed boat   a. tunic

2. .... to call for the presence of someone   b. gild(ed)

3. .... claws; usually of a bird of prey   c. coax(ed)

4. .... to persuade or convince   d. scoff(ed)

5. .... a loud noise   e. Memphis

6. .... an unmarried girl or woman   f. talons

7. .... to pay attention; to notice   g. din

8. .... to cover with a thin layer of gold   h. maiden

9. .... modern day Cairo; a city on the Nile   i. heed

10. .... a simple slip-on article of clothing   j. summon(ed)

11. .... to mock or make fun of   k. barge

Name _____ Class _____ Date _____

The Egyptian Cinderella
by Shirley Climo / illustrated by Ruth Heller

ADJECTIVE: a word used to modify a noun or a pronoun (for example, nimble)
NOUN: a word used to name a person, place, thing, or idea (for example, river)
VERB: a word used to express action or a state of being (for example, summon)

Sort each italicized word into the correct column according to how it is used in the phrase.

royal barge	*servant* girls	Amasis *searched*	beautiful *slippers*
did not *heed* her	dance like a *stork*	girls *gawked*	You *splattered* mud
dainty slippers	clumsy *sandals*	he *commanded*	Horus *sends* me a sign
stolen by *pirates*	breeze *blew*	*mighty* bird	*Rhodopis* pretended
distant city	*rose-red* slipper	of the *falcon*	*winked* and *sparkled*
rosy gold	plain *tunic*		

ADJECTIVE   NOUN   VERB

Name _____ Class _____ Date _____

The Egyptian Cinderella
by Shirley Climo / illustrated by Ruth Heller

MONTAGE — a group of various items related to one topic.

> 1. Your teacher will assign you to a partner or into a group to create a montage about *The Egyptian Cinderella*.
>
> 2. The montage will be done on large poster paper. Put the names of the students who work on your montage on the front of your poster and include the title and author of the book.
>
> 3. Use at least six of the items below and check off the boxes of the ones that you use.
>
> 4. Label each item and write a caption explaining how it relates to *The Egyptian Cinderella*.
>
> 5. Present your montage to your classmates.

☆ Rhodopis (the main character)

☆ something that shows a Cinderella motif

☆ the Nile River (part of the setting)

☆ the servant girls (characters)

☆ animals in the story

☆ Amasis (an important character)

☆ plants and/or flowers of Egypt

☆ something that shows the setting of the story (ancient Egypt)

☆ an important incident from the plot of the story

☆ a symbol of ancient Egypt

Suggestions

Plan what to include on your montage and list the items as you plan. If you intend to bring items or materials from home, or print out pictures, labels, titles, or captions from your own computer, be sure to write a reminder in your homework assignment book. Decide how you will present your poster to the class and practice what you will say. Speak clearly and look at your classmates as you talk about your work. It usually works best if two persons hold the poster and one student presents.

A montage is most effective when it includes a variety of colors and textures. The strong verbs and descriptive adjectives used by author Shirley Climo help the reader or listener to imagine the story. The illustrations by Ruth Heller are colorful and not only help to tell the story in picture form, but also reveal details about life in ancient Egypt. Materials that can be used to make effective montages include cloth, aluminum foil, beads, dried flowers, colorful magazine cutouts, ribbon, wrapping paper, tissue paper, lightweight jewelry (that can be attached to a poster with a staple or tape), printouts from Internet photos, and letters and words made with markers, construction paper, chalk, pencil, ink or designed and printed from a computer.

Jouanah
A Hmong Cinderella
adapted by Jewell Reinhart Coburn with Tzexa Cherta Lee
illustrated by Anne Sibley O'Brien

Dr. Jewell Reinhart Coburn has adapted this centuries-old Hmong folktale from a story entitled "The Poor Girl" introduced by Blong Xiong as well as from oral traditions from Tzexa Cherta Lee's family. She first met some of the Hmong people when visiting Southeast Asia in the 1960's. Tzexa Cherta Lee is of Hmong ancestry, has worked as a writer and translator, and is now residing in St. Paul, Minnesota. The illustrator of this book is well-known for her two *Talking Walls* books and was introduced to the Hmong people when her parents worked at Ban Vinai refugee camp in Thailand. Anne Sibley O'Brien's authentic illustrations reveal the lovely, dramatic, and vibrant colors and patterns that are highly esteemed by these hard-working Hmong people who treasure things of beauty as well as the values of loyalty, kindness and freedom. The story of Jouanah comes to us from Southeast Asia where the Hmong people have lived in the the high mountains of Laos since fleeing the Hunan province of China in the 1800's. In the 1970's, again they fled their homes as communists sought revenge for the help these peoples gave to the Americans in the Vietnamese conflict.

After Jouanah's father is tricked at the market where he has gone to buy a much-needed cow and fails to come home with one, her mother offers to turn herself into a cow to assist the family. With the help of the cow, the farm prospers but the farmer, instead of returning his wife to her former self, takes a new wife who has an unpleasant daughter by the name of Ding. The new wife finds that the cow is helping Jouanah by spinning silk thread on her horns and pretends to be a tree spirit who requires that the silk be destroyed. The cow dies of sadness before her husband can follow the new wife's commands to kill her, but her spirit stays in a piece of cowhide stored in a sewing basket. She helps her daughter obtain a lovely skirt, blouse, purse, necklace, and tiny shoes to go to the New Year festivities. Jouanah's beauty and lovely clothes attract the attention of Shee-Nang who later finds her lost shoe and begins the traditional search for its owner.

The story ends with the stepmother trying to trick the young man into paying attention to her daughter instead of her stepdaughter, but Jouanah and Shee-Nang know their own hearts and leave together taking only the magic sewing basket. They marry and live long and joyful lives while the stepmother and Ding continue to create their own miseries. The magic cowhide awaits the births of the couple's descendants and will continue to protect and help those children.

Jouanah
A Hmong Cinderella
adapted by Jewell Reinhart Coburn with Tzexa Cherta Lee / illustrated by Anne Sibley O'Brien

MOTIFS AND IDEAS

📖 a magic cow helps Jouanah

📖 Jouanah's father is easily tricked and eventually dies

📖 a piece of soft cowhide helps Jouanah and a bull's tail helps Becan

📖 there is a cruel stepmother and one lazy stepsister

📖 a magic sewing basket helps her dress for the festival

📖 needlework, music, and dancing are important

📖 a search for the owner of a lost shoe

📖 Jouanah marries a good young man

CONNECTIONS

Using atlases, encyclopedias, and/or Internet websites, research the following:

- ★ story cloth
- ★ animism
- ★ Hmong people ("free people")
- ★ qeng
- ★ shaman
- ★ countries of Southeast Asia
- ★ list the countries
- ★ refugee camps
- ★ put the names on a blank map
- ★ Miao (Hunan province)

VOCABULARY WORDS

ancestors	exquisite	joss sticks	schemes
clutched	fretted	maiden	sulked
cowhide	incense	pebbles	vibrant

Choose the word that completes the sentence:

1. The shaman lit the .... and the smell of .... filled the air.

2. A synonym for worried is.. .

3. .... are the people from whom a person is descended.

4. In many folktales, a young unmarried woman is called a ....

5. Something (a person, a color, music) that is full of life is called ....

Jouanah
A Hmong Cinderella
adapted by Jewell Reinhart Coburn with Tzexa Cherta Lee / illustrated by Anne Sibley O'Brien

STORY CLOTH — Thousands of Hmong people fled Hunan province in China in the 1800's and came to the mountains of Laos to remain a "free people." Since the Hmong had no written language until the 1950's, they preserved their history and culture through large embroidered pieces of material called *story cloths*. The people, places, and actions shown on these story cloths helped to keep the history of the Hmong people alive. Anne Sibley O'Brien frames each written page of Jouanah with an oval illustration at the top and a colorful pattern design from traditional Hmong textile artwork at the bottom.

> Your teacher will assign you to work with your classmates to create a story cloth that tells the tale of Jouanah in picture form. When the pictures are finished, label them so that they can be taped together into quilt form in the order of the story's plot. Hmong textile designs and mazes can be used to make a border around the cloth. Although, a true *story cloth* has no written words, to make this classroom *story cloth* easier to follow, write a short description beneath each drawing.

Some of the places and incidents that can be illustrated are listed below:

1. the mountain village

2. the soup-drinking contest

3. winding the vines

4. wife becomes cow

5. cow magically spins silk

6. Jouanah is given all the hard work

7. new wife hides in tree and tricks the farmer

8. silken thread is thrown into the fire

9. cow dies of broken heart

10. Jouanah is ordered to clean rice

11. magic sewing basket produces skirt, blouse, purses, necklace, and shoes

12. Jouanah arrives at the festival

13. Shee-Nang plays the qeng for the lovely young maiden

14. Jouanah loses a shoe to hurry home before her stepmother and stepsister

15. Shee-Nang finds the dainty shoe and Jouanah is afraid to try it on

16. Jouanah and Shee-Nang's eyes meet and hearts touch, and soon wed

17. Jouanah and Shee-Nang visit where the cow is buried

18. Jouanah and Shee-Nang live a long and joyful life together

Name _____ Class _____ Date _____

Jouanah
A Hmong Cinderella
adapted by Jewell Reinhart Coburn with Tzexa Cherta Lee / illustrated by Anne Sibley O'Brien

Each arm of the star shown below is labeled with different parts of speech. Sort the words listed below by putting each of them into or around the arm where the word belongs.

radiant	deceitful	exquisite	ancestors	tree	strutted
pebbles	pressed	incense	sulked	basket	sun-splashed
Jouanah	slyly	farmer	Ding	new	forest's edge
sit	shoes	muddy	village	searched	kicked
mysterious	stepmother	mournfully	wife	sadly	joyously
rock	Shee-Nang	sweetly	loving	care	eyes
jungle	sadness	cow	the market		

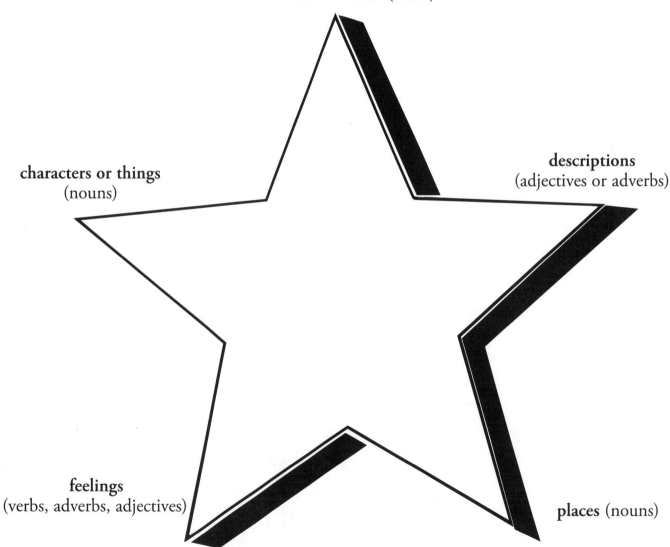

action words (verbs)

characters or things (nouns)

descriptions (adjectives or adverbs)

feelings (verbs, adverbs, adjectives)

places (nouns)

The Persian Cinderella
by Shirley Climo / illustrated by Robert Florczak

Writer and folklorist Shirley Climo adds to her list of Cinderella stories from around the world with the publication of *The Persian Cinderella*. This richly worded and designed book brings the reader into the exotic world of 15th century Persia where many things are very different but some things are the same. Artist Robert Florczak uses a combination of bright lush colors and meticulously researched patterns which complement and add to this beautifully worded tale from *The Arabian Nights*.

Settareh, whose name means "star," lives in long ago Persia, a land of princes and poets. And she learns to love a poetical prince who explains that the star scar on her face is "heaven-sent." As usual in these tales, the Cinderella character lives with a stepmother and two stepsisters who mistreat her. Settareh's father is alive but seldom visits the women's quarters and is usually too busy to give her much attention. However, he does give her a gold coin to buy cloth for new clothes to celebrate *No Ruz*, the Middle Eastern New Year. But Settareh fails to purchase cloth. Instead she buys something delicious to eat, kindly gives money to an old crone, and then sees a lovely blue jug which she finds desirable and buys with her last coins. Of course there is a helper in the form of a *pari* who lives in the jug, a festival where Settareh is noticed by Prince Mehrdad, and the losing of an article of clothing. This time it's an anklet that will only fit over Settareh's foot but it's the prince's mother who goes from home to home, riding in a palanquin, to find its owner.

Rather than ending the story with a wedding right after Settareh meets her prince, Leila and Nahid manage to use the magical blue jug to turn their stepsister into a turtledove. The prince eventually rescues Settareh when he kindly removes the hairpins from the turtledove's feathers and she metamorphasizes back into her original form. There is a wedding and happiness for Settareh and Prince Mehrdad at the end of the tale, but the stepsisters cause their own destruction when their jealousy and rage cause their hearts to burst.

The Persian Cinderella
by Shirley Climo / illustrated by Robert Florczak

MOTIFS AND IDEAS

📖 this version is 15th century Persia which is today's Iran

📖 Settareh lives with stepmother, two stepsisters, aunts & cousins

📖 father is alive but doesn't have very much time for Settareh

📖 the fairy "helper" is called a pari and lives in a jug

📖 there is a festival and Settareh loses her anklet

📖 stepsisters' vices cause their own deaths

📖 a wedding ceremony at the end

CONNECTIONS

The Artist's Note at the back of the book states that he has researched the costume, architecture, props, designs, color schemes, landscape, flora and fauna of ancient Persia in creating the illustrations for *The Persian Cinderella*. Describe some details about the pictures that confirm this:

....

....

....

....

....

VOCABULARY WORDS

arcade	ebony	pari	rushlights	bangle	*No Ruz*
turban	sash	bazaar	palanquin	quarters	pomogranite

Choose the word that matches its meaning:

1. .... Persian holiday for New Year   a. rushlights

2. .... headdress made of a long cloth   b. turban

3. .... black; dark   c. bangle

4. .... a light made from rushes and grease   d. palanquin

5. .... assigned place to live   e. ebony

6. .... a covered litter to carry someone   f. pari

7. .... a bracelet or anklet   g. quarters

8. .... a Persian fairy (usually helpful to humans) h. *No Ruz*

Name _____ Class _____ Date _____

The Persian Cinderella
by Shirley Climo / illustrated by Robert Florczak

QUICKWRITE

Before your teacher reads you the story, look at the illustration on the cover and list three unusual things that you notice:

....

....

CLARIFY

When your teacher stops reading, write down one word or idea that you need explained:

....

....

QUESTION

Write one question about the story: (Begin with one of these words: Why, Who, When, What, or Where)

....

....

PREDICT

After your teacher reads the part where the little blue jug shatters and six jeweled hairpins glitter on the floor, predict what will happen next:

....

....

SUMMARIZE

When you have finished listening to the story, write a one paragraph summary of the story. Include the setting, main characters, what happened (the plot), and the ending or resolution of the story. Use complete sentences:

....

....

....

....

....

EVALUATE

What did you like best about this Cinderella story?

....

....

....

The Persian Cinderella
by Shirley Climo / illustrated by Robert Florczak

ACROSS

2. In ancient Persia, a fairy who often helped humans was called a ....
5. A bright red fruit, the color of Settareh's silk dress
8. An example of "metamorphosis" is when Settareh is turned into a ....
9. A wide piece of cloth worn around the waist.
10. The stepsisters put these into Settareh's hair.
11. Prince .... says that the star on Settareh's face is "heaven-sent."
13. The second stepsister is called ....
16. An old woman is sometimes referred to as a ....
17. The pari lives in the little blue ....
18. Prince Mehrdad wears a .... on his head.

DOWN

1. Another name for a marketplace is ....
3. The Prince's mother rode in a litter called a ....
4. This name means "star."
5. At their wedding, the couple was showered with ne thousand matched ....
6. To avoid embarrassment, Settareh looks at the reflection of the prince in a ....
7. The name of the older stepsister is ....
12. A bangle or piece of jewelry worn around the ankle is called an ....
13. The Persian name for New Year is ....
14. In Persia, Women covered their heads with a ....
15. Today's name for ancient Persia is ....

The Rough-Face Girl
by Rafe Martin / illustrated by David Shannon

The dark and mysterious book cover of The *Rough-Face Girl* is enough by itself to create interest in this Algonquin Native American Indian tale. David Shannon shows a young girl whose face is hidden behind bandaged hands and whose one eye sends a message of pain. Her ragged clothing and the feather behind her hair give clues to a story that needs to be told. Caldecott-winner David Shannon's interest in Native Americans is obvious and his illustrations are haunting in their beauty. Professional storyteller Rafe Martin unfolds this story of goodness rewarded in a way that reinforces the universal values revealed by the tale.

As usual the central character of this tale is a young girl who is mistreated, but this time it is by her own two sisters. While her mother is absent and probably dead, her father is alive, but ignores the cruelties inflicted by her sisters. In this Algonquin village there is a huge wigwam occupied by an Invisible Being and his sister. The Invisible Being is said to be wealthy and handsome but he will marry only a young woman who is able to see him. The Algonquin Cinderella character has been named Rough-Face by her sisters because not only her arms, hands, clothes, and hair have been damaged by sparks from the hearth-fire she must continually tend, but her face has also been scarred. Her haughty and proud sisters are sure they will be able to earn the privilege of marrying the Invisible Being but they fail the test of honesty by lying when asked for details about his appearance. The Rough-Face girl obtains some worn-out articles of clothing from her father and then makes other things for herself and sets off with courage and faith to test herself and see the Invisible Being. Her appreciation of the beauty of nature allows her to see the Invisible Being as his sister questions the Rough-Face girl about what his bow and sled runner are made from.

Both the sister and her brother recognize her inner beauty and before the marriage, she is given beautiful clothing and bathes in a lake that magically restores her natural beauty. The story ends with the point that the Invisible Being and his sister saw her inner goodness before her outward beauty could be seen.

The Rough-Face Girl
by Rafe Martin / illustrated by David Shannon

MOTIFS AND IDEAS

📖 The Rough-Face Girl is from an Algonquin Indian Cinderella tale

📖 the central character has two cruel sisters rather than stepsisters

📖 unlike other Cinderella stories, she's beautiful only on the inside

📖 her sisters call her Rough-Face because her face is scarred

📖 her sisters try to see the Invisible Being but fail

📖 the Rough-Face girl sees things as they are

📖 the helper is the Invisible One's sister

📖 ends with marriage and happiness

CONNECTIONS

Using atlases, encyclopedias, and/or Internet websites, research the following:

⭐ where the Algonquins lived   ⭐ clothing of Algonquins

⭐ importance of nature symbols   ⭐ way of life (food, housing)

VOCABULARY WORDS

ashamed	desperately	leggings	sigh(ed)
awesome	glossy	moccasins	stammer(ed)
buckskin	hard-hearted	quiver	vanished
charred	haughtily	runner	wigwam

Choose the word that completes the sentence:

1. After the fire, the wood on the outside of the house was ....and black.

2. If something has disappeared, it has ....

3. Often Native Americans wore .... made out of ....

4. In Cinderella stories the sisters or stepsisters are often proud and act ....

5. The young brave put arrows into his .... before leaving to hunt.

Name _____ Class _____ Date _____

The Rough-Face Girl
by Rafe Martin / illustrated by David Shannon

SYNONYM — a word that means almost the same thing as another word.

ANTONYM — a word that means the opposite of another word.

THESAURUS — a reference book that lists groups of words with similar meanings

Most dictionaries also include synonyms and antonyms for many of the entry words. Often these synonyms and antonyms are shown in capital letters.

> Listed below are some words used in The Rough-Face Girl. Write at least one synonym beside each of the words. Use a dictionary or thesaurus if you have trouble thinking of a word. Remember that a synonym is one word, not a phrase or group of words.

1. wigwam ....

2. huge ....

3. pictures ....

4. rich ....

5. marry ....

6. powerful ....

7. see ....

8. painted ....

9. swift ....

10. cruel ....

> Find an antonym for each of the following words from The Rough-Face Girl.

11. morning ....

12. cruel ....

13. sister ....

14. handsome ....

15. visible ....

Name _____ Class _____ Date _____

The Rough-Face Girl
by Rafe Martin / illustrated by David Shannon

> Each arm of the star shown below is labeled with different parts of speech. Sort the words listed below by putting each of them into or around the arm where the word belongs.

marry	women	rich	village	Invisible Being
sister	dress	hair	gently	stars
bow	stepped	black	kind	see
wise	gladness	wigwam	lakeshore	sled
beautiful	proud	necklaces	father	haughtily
insisted	swift	strong	lightning	huge
handsome	sweet	ugly	glossy	Rough-Face Girl
entrance	heard	lake	Milky Way	water's edge

action words (verbs)

characters or things (nouns)

descriptions (adjectives or adverbs)

feelings (verbs, adverbs, adjectives)

places (nouns)

The Turkey Girl
A Zuni Cinderella Story
retold by Penny Pollock / illustrated by Ed Young

The father of the author is a descendent of a Native American Indian chief which gave Penny Pollock a special interest in this Zuni Cinderella version. The illustrator of this story has won the Caldecott Medal for *Lon Po Po: A Chinese Little Red Riding Hood*, and two of his other books were Caldecott Honor Books. His dreamlike illustrations are a perfect match for this lesson-teaching legend of the importance of friendship and keeping ones word.

In ancient times, a young orphaned girl, living in a pueblo village, makes her living by herding the turkeys owned by the wealthy families of Matsaki. She is so poor that she lives by herself and is shunned by the other young girls, presumably because of her tattered clothing and poverty. Turkey Girl, as she is called, not only cares for and tends the turkeys, but also considers them her friends. As usual in these tales, there is a messenger (the herald-priest) who invites all to attend a festival called the Dance of the Sacred Bird in near-by Hawikuh. Turkey Girl imagines dancing at the festival and talks aloud of her dreams as she goes about caring for the turkeys. The Old One, a huge gobbler, surprises her by speaking to her in words she can understand, and then, he and the other turkeys create a lovely white doeskin dress, beaded moccasins, and a mantle decorated with turkey feathers out of her ragged clothing. Treasures in the form of jewelry for her to wear to the festival rain down from the gullets of the turkeys as they fly above Turkey Girl. Her friends only ask that she return to them before nightfall as proof that she hasn't forgotten them.

As usual with the dancing young women in these Cinderella stories, Turkey Girl gets carried away and forgets the time. But in this situation, her turkey friends have given her an important charge and proof of her word depends on her return before "Sun-Father returns to his sacred place." The conclusion of the tale is a sad one as Turkey Girl's clothing returns to its original form, and she sees by the moonlight that the turkeys have left the stockade and she is left without her only friends. The story concludes by suggesting that this tale accounts for turkeys living ever after away from their tall brothers — human beings.

Name _____ Class _____ Date _____

The Turkey Girl
A Zuni Cinderella Story
retold by Penny Pollock / illustrated by Ed Young

MOTIFS AND IDEAS

📖 many Native American Indian names and references

📖 central character is an orphan

📖 Turkey Girl's only friends are the turkeys she tends

📖 a festival (Dance of the Sacred Bird) is announced

📖 an older person offers help (the Old One)

📖 clothing and jewels change her appearance

📖 a test of worthiness

📖 an unusual ending

CONNECTIONS

Using an atlas, locate the following places and areas on a map of New Mexico. You may want to find more information about each using the Internet, travel agency materials, and/or geographical and travel reference books.

✯ town of Zuni   ✯ Zuni Indian Reservation   ✯ Continental Divide

✯ Hawikuh Ruins   ✯ Zuni Mountains

VOCABULARY WORDS

arroyo	commotion	gullet(s)	orphan(ed)
ceremonial	dangled	latched	tattered
clad	delicate	mantle	tend

Choose the word that matches its meaning:

1. .... locked   a. mantle

2. .... a stream in a dry place   b. tattered

3. .... dressed or clothed   c. commotion

4. .... throat or esophagus   d. latched

5. .... a child with no parents   e. gullet

6. .... a loose sleeveless garment   f. ceremonial

7. .... ragged and torn   g. clad

8. .... to hang loosely   h. arroyo

9. .... excitement or confusion   i. dangled

10. .... belonging to a ceremony   j. orphan

Name _____ Class _____ Date_____

The Turkey Girl
A Zuni Cinderella Story
retold by Penny Pollock / illustrated by Ed Young

> This Native American Cinderella folktale is different from most of the other tales in that it does not end in the usual familiar and comforting way. After listening carefully to the story (or rereading it on your own), think about the story, and write about it on the lines below.

1. Did you predict that this story would not have the usual happy ending? Why did you predict it or why were you surprised?

....

....

2. The Turkey Girl thinks of the turkeys as her friends. Humans are described as the turkeys' *tall brothers*. How do these ideas fit in with what you know about Native American beliefs?

....

....

3. The Turkey Girl must come back to Matsaki "before the Sun-Father returns to his sacred place." Explain the words that are in quotations.

....

....

4. The illustrations in this book were done in oil crayon and pastel. Why do you think the creators of this book selected this technique? How do you think the illustrations help tell the story?

....

....

5. What is your favorite part of this book?

....

....

6. Did you like or dislike the ending? Explain.

....

....

....

....

Name _____ Class _____ Date _____

The Turkey Girl
A Zuni Cinderella Story
retold by Penny Pollock / illustrated by Ed Young

SYNONYM — a word that means almost the same thing as another word.

ANTONYM — a word that means the opposite of another word.

THESAURUS — a reference book that lists groups of words with similar meanings.

Most dictionaries also include synonyms and antonyms for many of the entry words. Often these synonyms and antonyms are shown in capital letters.

> Listed below are some words used in The Turkey Girl. Write at least one synonym beside each of the words. Use a dictionary or thesaurus if you have trouble thinking of a word. Remember that a synonym is one word, not a phrase or group of words.

1. hut ....
2. village ....
3. wealthy ....
4. dawn ....
5. festival ....
6. gobbler ....
7. unlocked ....
8. raced ....
9. proud ....
10. sorrow ....

> Find an antonym for each of the following words from The Turkey Girl.

11. dawn ....
12. proud ....
13. unlocked ....
14. sorrow ....
15. poor ....
16. shortens ....

Yeh-Shen
A Cinderella Story From China
retold by Ai-Ling Louie / illustrated by Ed Young

Caldecott Book Winner Ed Young researched the story of Yeh-Shen in two trips to China—the country of his birth. His dreamlike illustrations capture the story beautifully. On each page is a symbol or an illustration of the carp fish who befriends and helps Yeh-Shen. The author, Ai-Ling Louie, remembers hearing the story from her grandmother and discovered that the tale has been told in China for over a thousand years. A block-printed page from a Chinese edition is included in this book and the Chinese writing is something that could be researched through books and the Internet.

A cave chief of southern China by the name of Wu has two wives who each give birth to a baby girl. One of the wives grows sick and dies. Soon Wu also dies. Their small daughter is left orphaned and in the care of her stepmother and soon her beauty, goodness, and intelligence create feelings of jealousy as Yeh-Shen's stepsister has none of these gifts. The young girl befriends an enormous fish and often gives it food, but when her stepmother discovers this small pleasure, she tricks the fish, and then kills and cooks it for dinner. A wise old man (a sage) reveals to Yeh-Shen how the fish has disappeared but tells her not to dwell on the past, but to appreciate that the fish has a powerful spirit which will know her heart's desire and give her gifts. Yeh-Shen is helped by the fish bone's spirit and eventually attends a festival dressed in an azure blue gown, a cloak of kingfisher feathers, and tiny golden slippers. She attracts much attention, but loses one of the shoes as she flees when it appears that her stepsister might recognize her.

The lovely slipper eventually reaches the king who is determined to find its owner. Many of the countryside cave women try on the shoe and fail to prove it is theirs. It is not until the king sees Yeh-Shen slipping into the pavilion in the darkness of night, that he finds the lovely and good owner of the shoe. The end of the story tells of marriage and happiness for Yeh-Shen, but also reveals that fate deals harshly with her stepmother and stepsister when they are crushed in a shower of stones.

Name _____ Class _____ Date _____

Yeh-Shen
A Cinderella Story From China
retold by Ai-Ling Louie / illustrated by Ed Young

MOTIFS AND IDEAS

📖 the oldest known Cinderella story; from the T'ang dynasty (618-907 A.D.)

📖 Yeh-Shen's father had two wives and two daughters

📖 parents die and Yeh-Shen is raised by her cruel stepmother

📖 her helper is a fish who is killed by the stepmother

📖 an older man (a sage) gives Yeh-Shen advice

📖 there is a festival and Yeh-Shen loses her slipper

📖 the king marries the owner of the slipper

📖 "fate" punishes at the end

CONNECTIONS

The wise old man (called a "sage" in the story) gives Yeh-Shen this advice as he tells her that her stepmother has killed the girl's fish-friend: "Let us not dwell on things that are past ... ." Think about why sometimes it's best to put aside past evils or problems. Write about a time when you decided to leave the past behind:

....

....

....

....

VOCABULARY WORDS

azure	dynasty	herald	sage
collapse(d)	enormous	marvel(ed)	sweetmeats
crafty	filthy	pavilion	transformed
dread	heaved	predates	vigil

Choose the word that matches its meaning:

1. .... a building or tent used for festivals   a. vigil

2. .... an official messenger   b. azure

3. .... blue color of a clear sky   c. predates

4. .... a period of watching or wakefulness   d. pavilion

5. .... "before" the date   e. dynasty

6. .... a powerful group or family   f. herald

Name _____ Class _____ Date _____

Yeh-Shen
A Cinderella Story From China
retold by Ai-Ling Louie / illustrated by Ed Young

> 1. After reading or listening to Yeh-Shen, complete the information below.
>
> 2. The "I thought ..." section should be written in complete sentences and you should use every line.
>
> 3. In the area at the bottom of the page, draw an illustration with a caption (words explaining the picture) of something that interested you from the story.

Country or Ethnic Group: ....

Hero or Heroine: ....

Description of family: ....

A conflict or hardship: ....

Event helper: ....

Test of worthiness: ....

Use of magic: ....

Resolution: ....

I thought this story: ....

....

....

....

Yeh-Shen
A Cinderella Story From China
retold by Ai-Ling Louie / illustrated by Ed Young

In the olden days in China it was considered very desirable for a woman to have small feet. In many of the Cinderella stories, one of the things that is noticeable about the sandal, slipper or shoe that the central character loses is that it is very tiny. Chinese American poet Janet S. Wong tells a story of how her grandmother grew tired of her granddaughter's fussiness and complaints when they went to the mall looking for new athletic shoes. Grandmother (Popo) told Janet about the suffering that small girls in China used to endure and later Janet reflected on the incident and wrote a poem about it:

Bound Feet

Smoothing her fingers,
Popo shows how, back in China, long ago
they used to roll young girls' feet,
soaked in salt for softer bones,
rolled and rolled and rolled and tied
in packages of tender meat.

Hearing that, I like my feet.

> Beside each word or phrase, write a comment or a sentence or two about how, even today, people often value appearances more than they should.

name brand clothes

....

....

popularity

....

....

shoes that are uncomfortable

....

....

sagging

....

....

color of skin

....

....

ANSWER KEYS
Abadeha: The Philippine Cinderella

CONNECTIONS (p.12)
An Internet search using Google will bring up some sites that actually show samples of Alebeta writing. Students will also find that the art of this ancient writing is being revived in parts of the Philipines today.

VOCABULARY (p.12)

1. hammock
2. betel
3. solace
4. ancestors
5. radiant
6. mock

QUICKWRITE (p.13)
If students have difficulty coming up with ideas, brainstorm and list as students contribute.

VISUALIZE IT (p.13)
Students may need some guidance on how to come up with a caption. Explain that a caption for a picture can be a comment about what is shown, a mini-title for the illustration, or a brief description of what is drawn.

CHARACTER TYPES (p.14)
Cinderella: Angkat; Domitila; Settareh; Abadeha.
Helper: the falcon; Spirit of the Forest; godmother (Nannin); The Old One; Baba Yaga; the pari.
Prince Charming: the invisible warrior; the son of the island chieftain; Shee-Nang; the magistrate.

Angkat: The Cambodian Cinderella

VOCABULARY (p.16)
1. sarong 2. hoist(ed) 3. destiny 4. inlet 5. concoct(ed) 6. sampot 7. multitude 8. mystical
9. dawdle(d) 10. banish(ed) 11. iridescent

SORTING WORDS (p.17)
pronouns: I, his, She, you, he, her, My, They, it
adverbs: gracefully, lightly, carefully, quickly, instantly, forever, abundantly
prepositions: in, with, to, under, without, by

PREPOSITIONAL POEM (p.18)
Answers will vary. Suggestion: have students add more prepositions to the list on the worksheet. Lists of prepositions can be found in most language arts texts as well as in dictionaries. It may be useful to model a Prepositional Poem on the overhead using contributions from the class and using a student or another character from Angkat or from another folk or fairy tale as the topic of the poem.

Anklet for a Princess: A Cinderella Story from India

CONNECTIONS (p.20)

Yam Festival (Ghana & Nigeria)
Succoth (Israel)
Pongal (India)
Thanksgiving (United States & Canada)

Harvest Home (British Isles)
Hounen Odori (Japan)
Crop Over/Sugar Cane (Barbados)
Birthday of the Moon (China)

VOCABULARY (p.20)

1. pomegranate
2. marquee
3. sputter
4. aromas
5. sari
6. conch
7. fetch

QUICKWRITE (p.21)
Answers will vary. Suggestion: If your students are not familiar with this reading comprehension technique, you will need to review each term and model examples. Students will need this worksheet in front of them as you read or reread the story to them. Stop after a couple of pages so that students may complete the CLARIFY section.

LEARNING TO RESEARCH (p.22)
Facts about king cobras that students may find include the following: smells using its tongue; often lives near water, has false eyespots on the back of its head; life span is about 20 years; the only snake that

builds a nest and stays with the eggs; feeds on other snakes, small rodents, and lizards; swallows its prey head first; carnivore (meat-eater); average king cobra is 13 feet (4 meters) long; throat is light yellow or cream-colored; kills by biting and spitting venom up to eight feet; the venom is called neuratoxin; sheds skin four to six times a year; drinks lots of water when shedding skin; fangs are almost 1/2 inch long; excellent sight; responds to "snake charmers" through visual cues.

WHERE DID I FIND THESE FACTS

The important thing to teach children of all ages is that when information is found and used, credit must be given to the person or organization that published the information. A good way to verify that a piece of information is correct is to find the same fact in more than one place. Below is a SIMPLIFIED format for elementary school children to use when citing sources:

Newspaper: Smith, James. "Swimming With Crocodiles." Olean Times Herald. December 12, 2002.

Magazine: Nguyen, Thuy. "Table Tennis, A Lifetime Sport." Table Tennis World. January 2, 2003.

Book: Diaz, Thomas. Snakes of Western Canada. 2000.

Website: Center for Science Studies. "The Rings of Saturn." February 22, 2003. <www.cforss.org>

Baba Yaga & Vasilisa the Brave

VOCABULARY (p.24)

1. compassionate   2. gruesome   3. sinister   4. idle   5. chaff   6. ravenous   7. whim   8. menial   9. tzar
10. mortar & pestle

DESCRIPTION AND DRAWING (p.25)

Country or Ethnic Group: Russia

Hero or Heroine: Vasilisa

Description of family: mother has died, father remarried and then died, mean-spirited stepmother, her two daughters

A conflict or hardship: stepmother mistreats Vasilisa; sends her off into the forest to get light from Baba Yaga; Baba Yaga sets difficult tasks for Vasilisa but her doll helps her complete them

Event helper: the doll given to Vasilisa by her mother before she died; the old woman who takes her in after Vasilisa's stepmother and stepsisters are destroyed

Test of worthiness: Vasilisa completes the tasks for Baba Yaga; Vasilisa weaves beautiful cloth and gives it to the kind old woman ... the cloth eventually leads Vasilisa to the Tzar

Use of magic: Baba Yaga, the three horseman, the skull

Resolution: the Tzar finds the woman who has made the lovely cloth, falls in love with her and they marry; Vasilisa keeps her little friend the doll who represents her mother's love

PLOT (p.26)

Introduction: Baba Yaga is introduced on the 1st page; the main character's family is described; we learn about the doll

Rising Action: the stepmother sends Vasilisa for light; Vasilisa sees the three horsemen; Vasilisa finds Baba Yaga's house; the doll helps Vasilisa with her tasks; Baba Yaga gives the skull to Vasilisa

The Climax: the stepmother and stepsisters are destroyed

Falling Action: an elderly woman takes Vasilisa into her home; Vasilisa learns to spin and weave; the tzar sends for the person who made the cloth

Resolution: Vasilisa marries the tzar

Cendrillon: A Caribbean Cinderella

VOCABULARY (p.28)

1. manioc   2. calico   3. Caribbean Sea   4. chaperone   5. christening   6. Martinique
7. mahogany   8. peasant

QUICKWRITE (p.29)

Answers will vary. Suggestion: If your students are not familiar with this reading comprehension technique, you will need to review each term and model examples. Students will need this worksheet in front of them as you read or reread the story to them. Stop after reading the first couple of pages so that students may complete the CLARIFY section and after the part where the godmother meets Cendrillon at the river so that they may complete the PREDICT section.

COMPARE AND CONTRAST (p.30)

Answers will vary. May include the following:

In The Persian Cinderella: borders of Persian fabric designs, realistic colorful illustrations, central character is Settareh, story takes place in ancient Persia (present day Iran), women wear veils, Settareh loses an anklet, stepsisters are Leila and Nahid, a pari lives in a little blue jug, a festival for the New Year (No Ruz), Settareh marries Prince Mehrdad

In the intersected section of the Venn diagram: mothers die, artwork is brightly colored and very detailed, both central characters are mistreated by stepfamilies, both stories include magical objects, both stories include sherbert, both end with a marriage

In Cendrillon: borders of colorful plants and flowers, artwork is unusual, colorful, looks like oil with scratches, central character is Cendrillon, setting is an island in the Caribbean, clothes: look like the 1800's, women wear scarves tied around their hair, Cendrillon loses a pink slipper, stepsister's name is Vitaline, a mahogany wand, food: figs, apricots, roast lamb, cucumbers, rhubarb, a ball is given as a birthday fet, Cendrillon marries Paul Thiboult

Domitila: A Cinderella Tale from the Mexican Tradition

CONNECTIONS (p.32)

Aesop's The Fox and the Grapes (the fox decides that the grapes are sour when he cannot get them)

Aesop's The Town Mouse and the Country Mouse (the Country Mouse decides the plain food she eats is better than that which the Town Mouse for which she risks her life)

King Midas and the Golden Touch (even food is turned to gold)

Greek Myth of Demeter (Persephone eats the seeds of the pomegranate)

Bible (Old Testament) (Adam entices Eve to bite from the apple)

The White Snake (a ring in the fish)

VOCABULARY (p.32)

1. passed away 2. buenos dias 3. casa 4. deeds 5. serape 6. cunning 7. abuela 8. smirk

EXAMINING AND EXPLAINING A PROVERB (p.33)

Answers will vary. It may be necessary to take one of the proverbs and brainstorm and model with the class.

PRACTICING ANALOGIES (p.34)

1. Timoteo 2. good day 3. mansion 4. mountains 5. fiesta 6. arrogant 7. tortillas 8. kind 9. Mexico 10. shawl

The Egyptian Cinderella

VOCABULARY (p.36)

1. barge 2. summon(ed) 3. talons 4. coax(ed) 5. din 6. maiden 7. heed 8. gild(ed) 9. Memphis 10. tunic 11. scoff(ed)

SORTING WORDS (p.37)

nouns: slippers, stork, tunic, sandals, sign, pirates, Rhodopis, falcon

adjectives: royal, servant, dainty, distant, rose-red, mighty, rosy

verbs: searched, heed, dance, splattered, commanded, gawked, winked, sparkled, sends, blew, pretended

Jouanah: A Hmong Cinderella

VOCABULARY (p.40)

1. joss sticks, incense 2. fretted 3. Ancestors 4. maiden 5. vibrant

MAKING A STORY CLOTH (p.41)

Suggestions: Reading Dia's Story Cloth by Dia Cha would be a good introduction to this project; asking students to number their completed squares will help to keep the story in order for patching together.

WORKING WITH PARTS OF SPEECH (p.42)
(There may be some variation in the words placed under descriptions and feelings.)
action words: strutted, pressed, searched, sit, kicked, sulked
descriptions: radiant, muddy, deceitful, new, exquisite, sun-splashed, slyly,
feelings: mournfully, sweetly, sadness, sadly, loving, mysterious, joyously, care
places: village, jungle, forest's edge, the market
characters or things: basket, Ding, stepmother, rock, eyes, pebbles, Jouanah, Shee-Nang, wife, ancestors, incense, cow, tree, farmer, shoes

The Persian Cinderella

VOCABULARY (p.44)
1. No Ruz   2. turban   3. ebony   4. rushlights   5. quarters   6. palanquin   7. bangle   8. pari
QUICKWRITE (p.45)
Answers will vary. Suggestion: If your students are not familiar with this reading comprehension technique, you will need to review each term and model examples. Students will need this worksheet in front of them as you read or reread the story to them. Stop after reading the first couple of pages so that students may complete the CLARIFY section and after the part where the little blue jug shatters so that they may complete the PREDICT section.
CROSSWORD PUZZLE (p.46)

The Rough-Face Girl

VOCABULARY (p.48)
1. charred   2. vanished   3. moccasins, buckskin   4. hard-hearted   5. quiver
FINDING SYNONYMS (p.49)
Suggested answers: 1. wigwam (hut)   2. huge (large, enormous)   3. pictures (illustrations, images,

designs)   4. rich (wealthy, well-off)   5. marry (wed)   6. powerful (strong, forceful)   7.see (view, look)
8. painted (colored, decorated)   9. swift (quick, fast) 10. cruel (mean, fierce)
FINDING ANTONYMS
Suggested answers: 11. morning (evening, dusk)   12. cruel (kind, gentle)   13. sister (brother)
14. handsome (ugly, unpleasant)   15. visible (invisible, hidden)
WORKING WITH PARTS OF SPEECH (p.50)
(Answers may vary in the words placed under descriptions and feelings, things and places.)
action words: marry, insisted, stepped, heard, see
descriptions: wise, beautiful, handsome, swift, rich, black, strong, gently, kind, haughtily, huge, glossy
feelings: gladness,   proud, sweet,
places: entrance, wigwam, village, lakeshore, Milky Way, water's edge
characters or things: sister, bow, Invisible Being, dress, Rough-Face Girl, hair, necklace, lake, father,
lightning, women, stars, sled

The Turkey Girl

VOCABULARY (p.52)
1. latched 2. arroyo 3. clad 4. gullet 5. orphan 6. mantle 7. tattered 8. dangled   9. commotion
10. ceremonial
IDEAS TO THINK ABOUT (p.53)
Answers will vary. Suggestion: read the questions to the class (or parts of the questions as you probably
don't want to let the students know ahead of time that there is not the usual happy ending) before
reading the story aloud.
FINDING SYNONYMS (p.54)
Suggested answers: 1. hut (shack, shanty, shelter, house) 2. village (town, hamlet)   3. wealthy (rich,
prosperous) 4. dawn (sunrise, beginning, daybreak) 5. festival (party, feast, fair) 6. gobbler (turkey)
7. unlocked (open, unlatched) 8. raced (hurried, ran, sped) 9. proud (arrogant, haughty, disdainful)
10. sorrow (grief, anguish, regret
FINDING ANTONYMS (p.54)
Suggested answers: 11. dawn (dusk, sunset, ending)   12. proud (humble, meek, modest)
13. unlocked (closed, locked, latched) 14. sorrow (joy, happiness) 15. poor (rich, wealthy)
16. shortens (lengthens, enlarges)

Yeh-Shen: A Cinderella Story from China

VOCABULARY (p.56)
1. pavilion 2. herald 3. azure 4. vigil 5. predates 6. dynasty
DESCRIPTION & DRAWING (p.57)
Country or Ethnic Group: China
Hero or Heroine: Yeh-Shen
Description of family: mother and father died; raised by a stepmother who has a daughter
A conflict or hardship: stepmother mistreats Yeh-Shen; her fish friend is killed
Event helper: the old sage; spirit of the fish bones
Test of worthiness: Yeh-Shen always found something to share with the fish; tried to return the shoe to
the fish bone spirit; the tiny shoe fits only Yeh-Shen
Use of magic: spirit of the fish bones helps Yeh-Shen with clothes for the banquet; rags are transformed
into beautiful clothes
Resolution: Yeh-Shen marries the king; stepmother and stepsister are crushed to death
SOMETHING TO THINK & WRITE ABOUT (p.58)
Answers will vary. Suggestion: read the poem aloud and discuss ideas of beauty and how people value
appearances. After students think and write, share with the class or in small groups.

Twelve Cinderellas & Their DRP's

A DRP value is a unit of measurement used to:
1. measure the difficulty of text
2. report students' reading ability (for example, Charlotte's Web has a DRP value of 50. Students who have received DRP test scores of 50 are capable of reading Charlotte's Web and easier texts independently.)

Many fairy tales and other picture books obviously meant for young children have relatively high DRP text difficulty values. These books were not designed as beginning-to-read books. They were designed as read-aloud books. Such books have an important place in children's literacy development. The rich vocabulary and the complex structure of the sentences introduces the child to more sophisticated language than they are likely to hear in everyday conversation. The DRP scores for the twelve Cinderella stories we used in this guide are listed below:

Title	DRP
Abadeha: The Philippine Cinderella	56
Angkat: The Cambodian Cinderella	55
Anklet For a Princess: A Cinderella Story from India	53
Baba Yaga & Vasilisa the Brave	54
Cendrillon: A Caribbean Cinderella	50
Domitila: A Cinderella Tale from the Mexican Tradition	55
The Egyptian Cinderella	52
Jouanah: A Hmong Cinderella	55
The Persian Cinderella	55
The Rough-Face Girl	51
The Turkey Girl: A Zuni Cinderella Story	58
Yeh-Shen: A Cinderella Story from China	54

The above information is provided by
Touchstone Applied Science Associates (TASA), Inc.
TASA, Degrees of Reading Power and DRP are registered trademarks of
Touchstone Applied Science Associates, Inc.
More information can be obtained by visiting TASA's web site at www.tasaliteracy.com

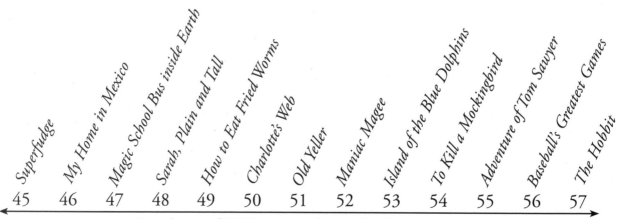

Correlation of DRP scores and some familiar titles